I'm Talking

Nura Azahar

Presentation by *BookLeaf Puhlishing*

Web: www.bookleafpub.com

E-mail: info@bookleafpub.com

ISBN : 9789357448109

First edition 2021

DEDICATION

To all the multiple versions of myself, you have grown and you will keep growing.

ACKNOWLEDGEMENT

The world is a better place thanks to people who pick others up when they feel down, the people who take you out to coffee when you don't want to get out of bed, the people that make you laugh when you don't feel like it and the home-cooked meal your mum makes that no other restaurant can replicate. I'd like to thank my family, my friends and my past and future self.

PREFACE

The poems have come to find you, find me, and sometimes they find people who are not looking for it. The words are a collection of feelings that you can interpret, however, you feel fit.

melody in your head

how do you write the melody that's playing in your head ?

the ticking of time, the rushing flow of thoughts

what do you do when all you want to do is lie in your bed?

i'm talking, I'm screaming.

it's more than this you say, it's more than waking up and going to work.

dissociating, and feeling like this all isn't real.

i'll try again, the hot water hits my neck.

clean fabric touches the bare of my skin

walking outside, the melody in my head is playing again.

I never made it out.

how do you write the melody that's playing in your head?

i can't be the only one

i wanted to forget everything.

the way the cells are dying,

the way it isn't replacing.

I cried in the bath tub at my own birthday party
for 1 hour.

a friend with the cutest fringe, unkept messy.

the softest heart.

another with trauma that she has not dealt with.
holding my hand saying, you can't do this. stay
with me, I can't be here without you.

but don't you understand I cannot be here.

i can't be the only one that feels this way. I feel
so small. I am screaming and I can't hear
myself.

no one can hear me. I can't make myself feel
less alone. I can't be the only one.

leaving

what makes you so sure that you're all I need?
i'm leaving

work, pay the bills, repeat

it hurts to be here when all I do is work and pay
the bills to live.
what is the point of this,
did God want this for us?
did he make beautiful trees to be cut down?
did he create vibrant birds to be shot out of the
sky?
did he create magnificent elephants for their
tusks to be displayed in a house that is dressed in
fur?
was his purpose for us to fall in love and be
taken away from us.
i still see your face when I close my eyes. I wish
I felt alive, I wish I was cut down, I wish I was
shot out of the sky, I wish I was displayed.
then at least I will feel something.

every time

every time you tell a woman to lower her voice
because she sounds bossy
you are confusing her with her attempt of
courage
every time you push a woman when you are
angry
you are confusing her perception of love
every time you make a promise to a woman and
break it
you are confusing her that promises mean
nothing
now she walks through life with a lowered
voice, paired with love that screams and pushes
her and with promises that are unkept.
every time this happens, a piece of her is
weeping.

golden

the sun will shine

and tan your skin

you complain that you are getting too dark

so you cover up and conceal your skin

you say "this will help me remain light"

that lipstick shade you saw on another girl

doesn't look too great on you

you say "it's because of how dark I am"

you don't realise it's them that need to cater for
your beauty

as you are covering your golden light.

yell help

i had all, then some of you, and then none of you

if someone told me you were going to be gone
tomorrow

i don't know what I'm supposed to do

i have appreciated you but not how you wanted
me to

can you please see I am doing everything I can
for you

get better

you will wake up in the morning, and you won't
know where you've been

the feeling of loneliness in the darkness and
coldness of the bare room

and it feels like you been away for a long time
but to you nothing has changed at all

and it feels like I've been with you but at the
same time i'm talking about you in a call

more

I look up to the sky
and I know you're still alive
it doesn't just end here
you are far too precious to die

glowing

the way that you see yourself

is not the way that people see you

you wouldn't see that in your friend

don't do that, you don't deserve to

I love, love

time is being spent

so valuable in its sense

you could not replace it
but if you could you would make it fit

into that hole,
of darkness and void

stop shutting them out
they're not that cold.

you say "I love, love. but I don't know if I can
love love if it has to do with me."

me

you can imitate me
but you will never be me

someone knows

slow down

i know you wanna understand
maybe I can explain it to you

i should let someone know
that something doesn't feel right

you think that you are okay
then you are not

i should let someone know
maybe when I am better

adhd

i brought an apple to school today

it was green and bright

did this make me happy?

as ordinary things do

just lately, i've been walking around with
thoughts in my head

they don't stop

these tasks keep piling up

working on three at the same time

the rest of the day was quite easy

i did all the jobs on my list

maybe i am glad that i do exist

just one more

i know it's so late, I know we're busy tomorrow,
I know we can watch it another time, but please,
just one more

i know we've eaten, I know I'll feel bad in the
morning, I know it's not good for me, but please
just one more

i know it still hurts, I know we haven't spoken
about it, I know I've had a thousand chances, but
please, just one more

i know your times up, I know the drugs make
you feel sick, I know you've only got days left,
but please, just one more

Just one more of anything with you

contrast

i am forgetful
you are reliable
i am emotional
you are dispassionate
i don't want to be here
you do

sadness is living in parts where it should not be

you have sadness in your eyes
you have sadness in your smile
you have sadness between your fingers when
you pull the sleeves of your sweater
you have sadness amongst a group of friends
but what you don't have is me
maybe that could change the sadness

show up

i've told you the time
i wanted you to be there
let me tell you harshly
i know we won't be fine
I am trying to be fair
but you are weighing me down